HEAR THE CALL

50 Songs of Missions and Evangelism

Compiled by Ken Bible

Lillenas PUBLISHING COMPANY
KANSAS CITY, MO 64141
www.lillenas.com

Song for the Nations

CHRIS CHRISTENSEN   CHRIS CHRISTENSEN

1. May we be a shin - ing light to the na - tions, A
2. May we bring a word of hope to the na - tions, A
3. May we be a heal - ing balm to the na - tions, A
4. May we sing a song of joy to the na - tions, A
5. May Your king - dom come to the na - tions, Your

shin - ing light to the peo - ples of the earth, Till the
word of life to the peo - ples of the earth, Till the
heal - ing balm to the peo - ples of the earth, Till the
song of praise to the peo - ples of the earth, Till the
will be done in the peo - ples of the earth, Till the

whole world sees the___ glo - ry of Your name.
whole world knows there's sal - va - tion thro' Your name.
whole world knows the___ pow - er of Your name.
whole world rings with the prais - es of Your name.
whole world knows that___ Je - sus Christ is Lord.

May Your pure light shine thro'___ us.
May Your mer - cy flow thro'___ us.
May Your heal - ing flow thro'___ us.
May Your song be sung thro'___ us.
May Your king - dom come in___ us.

2

Jesus Saves!

PRISCILLA J. OWENS   WILLIAM J. KIRKPATRICK

1. We have heard_____ the joy - ful sound: Je - sus saves! Je - sus
2. Waft in on_____ the roll - ing tide: Je - sus saves! Je - sus
3. Sing a - bove_____ the bat - tle strife: Je - sus saves! Je - sus
4. Give the winds_____ a might - y voice: Je - sus saves! Je - sus

saves! Spread the tid - ings all a - round: Je - sus
saves! Tell to sin - ners far and wide: Je - sus
saves! By His death_____ and end - less life, Je - sus
saves! Let the na - tions now re - joice: Je - sus

saves! Je - sus saves! Bear the news_____ to ev - 'ry
saves! Je - sus saves! Sing, ye is - lands of the
saves! Je - sus saves! Sing it soft - ly thro' the
saves! Je - sus saves! Shout sal - va - tion full and

land; Climb the steeps_____ and cross the waves. On - ward!
sea; Ech - o back,_____ ye o - cean caves. Earth shall
gloom, When the heart_____ for mer - cy craves; Sing in
free, High - est hills_____ and deep - est caves. This our

'tis_____ our Lord's com-mand. Je - sus saves! Je - sus saves!
keep_____ her ju - bi - lee. Je - sus saves! Je - sus saves!
tri - umph o'er the tomb: Je - sus saves! Je - sus saves!
song_____ of vic - to - ry: Je - sus saves! Je - sus saves!

Love Through Me

3

MOSIE LISTER   MOSIE LISTER

1. Love thro' me, love thro' me; O_____ Lord,
2. Weep thro' me, weep thro' me; O_____ Lord,
3. Speak thro' me, speak thro' me; O_____ Lord,

love thro' me. Some - where some - bod - y needs Your
weep thro' me. As_____ long as just one soul is
speak thro' me. Make Your Word up - on my lips a

love to - day. O Lord, love thro' me.
gone a - stray, O Lord, weep thro' me.
flame to - day. O Lord, speak thro' me.

4

Christ for the World We Sing

SAMUEL WOLCOTT   FELICE DE GIARDINI

1. Christ for the world we sing; The world to Christ we bring With loving zeal: The poor, and them that mourn, The faint and o-ver-borne, Sin-sick and sor-row-worn, Whom Christ doth heal.

2. Christ for the world we sing; The world to Christ we bring With fervent prayer: The way-ward and the lost, By rest-less pas-sions tossed, Re-deemed at count-less cost From dark de-spair.

3. Christ for the world we sing; The world to Christ we bring With one ac-cord: With us the work to share, With us re-proach to dare, With us the cross to bear, For Christ our Lord.

4. Christ for the world we sing; The world to Christ we bring With joy-ful song: The new-born souls whose days, Re-claimed from er-ror's ways, In-spired with hope and praise, To Christ be-long.

Lift Up the Cross

5

DENNIS and NAN ALLEN

DENNIS and NAN ALLEN

Lift up the cross!_____ Lift up the cross,_____ 'til ev-'ry

eye has__seen the Lamb of Cal - va - ry. Lift up the

cross!_____ Lift up the cross!_____ Ex - alt the

Son of God who__died, take up His cross and lift it__high, 'til ev-'ry

eye has seen the Lord,_____ Lift up the cross!____

6

People Need the Lord

GREG NELSON
and PHILL MCHUGH

GREG NELSON
and PHILL MCHUGH

Unison

1. Ev - 'ry day they pass me by, I can see it
2. We are called to take His light To a world where

in their eyes; Emp-ty peo-ple filled with care,
wrong is right; What could be too great a cost for

Head-ed who knows where. On they go thro'
Shar-ing life with one who's lost. Thro' His love our

pri - vate pain, Liv-ing fear to fear;
hearts can feel All the grief they bear;

Laugh-ter hides the si - lent cries_____ On-ly Je - sus
They must hear the words of life_____ On-ly we can

hears.
share. *Parts* Peo-ple need the Lord, Peo-ple need the

Lord; At the end of bro - ken dreams He's the o - pen

door._____ Peo-ple need the Lord, Peo-ple need the Lord;

When will we re - al - ize Peo-ple need the Lord.

7 Go Forth and Tell!

JAMES E. SEDDON   GEORGE W. WARREN

1. Go forth and tell! O
2. Go forth and tell! God's
3. Go forth and tell! Men
4. Go forth and tell! The
5. Go forth and tell! O

Church of God, a - wake!   God's sav - ing
love em - brac - es all;   He will in
still in dark - ness lie;   In wealth or
doors are o - pen wide.   Share God's good
Church of God, a - rise!   Go in the

news to all the na - tions take.   Pro - claim Christ
grace re - spond to all who call.   How shall they
want, in sin they live and die.   Give us, O
gifts; let no one be de - nied.   Live out your
strength which Christ your Lord sup - plies.   Go till all

Je - sus, Sav - ior, Lord, and King,
call if they have nev - er heard
Lord, con - cern of heart and mind—
life as Christ your Lord shall choose;
na - tions His great name a - dore,

That all the world His wor - thy__ praise may sing.
The gra - cious in - vi - ta - tion__ of His Word?
A love like Yours which cares for__ all man - kind.
Your ran - somed pow'rs for His sole__ glo - ry use.
And serve Him– Lord and King for - ev - er - more.

Called to All Nations

8

STEPHEN R. ADAMS
& CRAIG ADAMS

CRAIG ADAMS

We are called,_____ called to all na-tions; Called_____ to

teach His__ Word._____ Shar - ing His pow'r with

ev - 'ry gen - er - a - tion. We are called to serve the__ Lord!

9

Rescue the Perishing

FANNY J. CROSBY

WILLIAM H. DOANE

1. Res - cue the per-ish-ing; Care for the dy - ing; Snatch them in
2. Tho' they are slight-ing Him, Still He is wait - ing— Wait - ing the
3. Down in the hu-man heart, Crushed by the tempt - er, Feel - ings lie
4. Res - cue the per-ish-ing; Du - ty de-mands it. Strength for thy

pit - y from sin and the grave. Weep o'er the err - ing one;
pen - i - tent child to re - ceive. Plead with them ear-nest - ly;
bur - ied that grace can re - store. Touched by a lov-ing heart,
la - bor the Lord will pro-vide. Back to the nar-row way

Lift up the fall - en; Tell them of Je - sus, the
Plead with them gent - ly; He will for - give if they
Wak - ened by kind - ness, Chords that are bro - ken will
Pa - tient-ly win them; Tell the poor wan - d'rer a

REFRAIN

Might - y to Save.
on - ly be - lieve.
vi - brate once more. Res - cue the per-ish-ing; Care for the
Sav - ior has died.

dy - ing. Je - sus is mer - ci - ful; Je - sus will save.

Your Love Compels Me

10

DOUG HOLCK

DOUG HOLCK

Your love com - pels me, Lord, To give as You would give,

To speak as You would speak, To live as You would live.

Your love com - pels me, Lord, To see as You would see,

To serve as You would serve, To be what You would be.

11   Here I Am, Lord

DAN SCHUTTE   DAN SCHUTTE

1. I, the Lord of sea and sky, I have heard my people cry. All who dwell in dark and sin my hand will save. I who made the stars of night, I will make their darkness bright. Who will bear my

2. I, the Lord of snow and rain, I have borne my people's pain. I have wept for love of them. They turn a-way. I will break their hearts of stone, give them hearts for love a-lone. I will speak my

3. I, the Lord of wind and flame, I will tend the poor and lame. I will set a feast for them. My hand will save. Fin-est bread I will pro-vide till their hearts be sat-is-fied. I will give my

© 1981, Daniel L. Schutte and New Dawn Music, 5536 NE Hassalo, Portland, OR 97213. All rights reserved. Used by permission.

light to them?   Whom shall I send?
word to them.   Whom shall I send?
life to them.   Whom shall I send?

REFRAIN

Parts

Here I am, Lord.   Is it I, Lord?

___ I have heard you call-ing in the night.

___ I will go, Lord, if you lead me.

___ I will hold your peo-ple in my heart.

12   We've a Story to Tell to the Nations

H. ERNEST NICHOL

1. We've a sto - ry to tell to the na - tions That shall turn their hearts to the right, A sto - ry of truth and____ mer - cy, A sto - ry of peace and light,____ A sto - ry of peace and light.

2. We've a song to be sung to the na - tions That shall lift their hearts to the Lord, A song that shall con - quer____ e - vil And shat - ter the spear and sword,____ And shat - ter the spear and sword.

3. We've a mes - sage to give to the na - tions– That the Lord who reign - eth a - bove Hath sent us His Son to____ save____ us And show us that God is love,____ And show us that God is love.

4. We've a Sav - ior to show to the na - tions Who the path of sor - row hath trod, That all of the world's great____ peo - ples Might come to the truth of God,____ Might come to the truth of God.

For the dark - ness shall turn to dawn - ing, And the dawn - ing to noon - day bright, _____ And Christ's great king - dom shall come to earth– The king - dom of love and light.

Carry the Light

13

TWILA PARIS

TWILA PARIS

Car - ry _____ the light, (Car - ry _____ the light,) car - ry _____ the light. Go and tell the chil - dren

A♭
E♭/G
B♭sus
B♭
Fm/B♭
they are precious in His sight.
A♭/B♭
E♭
E♭/G
Gm7
E♭/G
A♭M9
Fm/B♭
A♭M7/B♭
Carry the light, (Carry the light,) carry the
Gm7
A♭
E♭/G
G7
light. Go and preach the gospel till there is no more
Cm
E♭/B♭
A♭
E♭/G
A♭
night. In the name of Jesus Christ,
A♭M7/B♭
Fm/B♭
A♭/B♭
1
E♭
A♭/B♭
2
E♭
carry the light.
light.

Seedtime and Harvest

14

BILL O'BRIEN

DICK ANTHONY

1. Seed - time and har - vest, Fields full of grain;
2. Lord of the har - vest, You taught us to pray;
3. Lord of the har - vest, I am a - ware

Sea - sons re - fresh - ing, Sun - shine and rain.
Send forth the la - bor-ors While it is day.
Peo - ple have bur - dens Some - one must share.

La - bors all end - ed, Our work will cease;
Night soon is com - ing, Our work will cease;
You are the an - swer For ev - 'ry need;

Lord of the har - vest, O grant the in - crease.
Lord of the har - vest, O grant the in - crease.
Use me, Lord Je - sus, In plant - ing the seed.

15 I'll Go Where You Want Me to Go

Stanza 1, MARY BROWN;
Stanza 2 & 3, CHARLES E. PRIOR

CARRIE E. ROUNSEFELL

1. It may___ not be on the moun - tain's height, Or
2. Per - haps___ to - day there are lov - ing words Which
3. There's sure - ly some - where a___ low - ly place In

o - ver the storm - y sea;___ It may not
Je - sus would have me speak;___ There may be
earth's har - vest fields so wide___ Where I may

be at the bat - tle's front My Lord will have need of
now, in the paths of sin, Some wan - d'rer whom I should
la - bor thro' life's short day For Je - sus, the Cru - ci -

me.___ But if by a still,___ small voice He
seek.___ O Sav - ior, if Thou___ wilt be my
fied.___ So, trust - ing my all to Thy ten - der

calls To paths that I do___ not know,___ I'll
Guide, Tho' dark and___ rug-ged the way,___ My
care, And know - ing Thou lov - est me,___ I'll

an - swer, dear Lord, with my hand___ in Thine, "I'll go where You
voice___ shall ech - o the mes - sage sweet, I'll say what You
do___ Thy will with a heart___ sin - cere. I'll be what You

REFRAIN

want me to go."___
want me to say.___ I'll go where You want me to go, dear Lord.
want me to be.___

O - ver moun - tain, or plain,___ or sea.___ I'll say what You

want me to say,___ dear Lord, I'll be what You want me to be.___

16

Lord of the Harvest

BILL O'BRIEN

DICK ANTHONY

1. Lord of the har - vest, the la-borers are so few,
2. Lord of the har - vest, en - gage Your church en - tire,
3. Lord of the har - vest, we pray now as You taught,

Lord of the har - vest, there's so much yet to do;
Lord of the har - vest, en - dow us with Your fire;
Lord of the har - vest, we go now as we ought;

Lord of the har - vest, time will not stand still,
Lord of the har - vest, en - no - ble all our ways,
Lord of the har - vest, in - crease the la-borers still,

Lord of the har - vest, with ho - ly pow - er fill.
Lord of the har - vest, grant strength to match our days.
Lord of the har - vest, with us Your pow - er fill.

Use Me

DEWITT JONES
and KIM JONES

DEWITT JONES
and KIM JONES

If You can use an-y-thing, Lord, You can use me.

If You can use an-y-thing, Lord, You can use me.

Take my hands, Lord, and my feet,

Touch my heart, Lord, speak thro' me. If You can

use an-y-thing, Lord, You can use me.

18 Go Light Your World

CHRIS RICE

CHRIS RICE

1. There is a can - dle in ev - 'ry soul,
2. Frus - trat - ed broth - er, see how he's tried to
3. We are a fam - 'ly whose hearts are blaz - ing.

Some burn - ing bright - ly, some dark and cold.
Light his own can - dle some oth - er way.
Let's raise our can - dles– light up the sky!

There is a Spir - it who brings a fire,
See now your sis - ter, she's been robbed and lied to,
Pray to our Fath - er in the name of Je - sus;

Ig - nites a can - dle and makes His home.
Still holds a can - dle with - out a flame.
Make us a bea - con in dark - est times.

Carry your can - dle, run to the dark - ness, Seek out the hope - less, con-fused and torn. Hold out your can - dle for all to see it, Take your can - dle, and go light your world._____ Take your can - dle, and go light your world.

Macedonia

19

ANNE ORTLUND

HENRY S. CUTLER

1. The vi - sion of a dy - ing world Is vast be - fore our
2. The sav - age hugs his god of stone And fears de - scent of
3. To - day, as un - der - stand - ing's bounds Are stretched on ev - 'ry
4. The warn - ing bell of judg - ment tolls, A - bove us looms the

eyes;_____ We feel the heart-beat of its need, We
night;_____ The cit - y dwell-er cring - es lone A -
hand,_____ O clothe Thy Word in bright, new sounds And
cross,_____ A - round are ev - er - dy - ing souls– How

hear its fee - ble cries. Lord Je - sus Christ, re -
mid the gar - ish light. Lord Je - sus Christ, a -
speed it o'er the land. Lord Je - sus Christ, em -
great, how great the loss! O Lord, con - strain and

vive Thy Church In this, her cru - cial hour!_____ Lord
rouse Thy Church To see their mute dis - tress!_____ Lord
pow - er us To preach by ev - 'ry means!_____ Lord
move Thy Church The glad news to im - part!_____ And

Je - sus Christ, a - wake Thy Church With Spir - it - giv - en pow'r.
Je - sus Christ, e - quip Thy Church With love and ten - der - ness.
Je - sus Christ, em - bold - en us In near and dis - tant scenes.
Lord, as Thou dost stir Thy Church, Be - gin with - in my heart.

Jesus Shall Reign

ISAAC WATTS

JOHN HATTON

1. Je - sus shall reign wher - e'er the sun
2. To Him shall end - less prayer be made,
3. Peo - ple and realms of ev - 'ry tongue
4. Let ev - 'ry crea - ture rise and bring

Does his suc - ces - sive jour - neys run;
And end - less prais - es crown His head.
Dwell on His love with sweet - est song,
His grate - ful hon - ors to our King;

His king - dom spread from shore to shore,
His name like sweet per - fume shall rise
And in - fant voic - es shall pro - claim
An - gels de - scend with songs a - gain,

Till moons shall wax and wane no more.
With ev - 'ry morn - ing sac - ri - fice.
Their ear - ly bless - ings on His name.
And earth re - peat the loud "A - men!"

21 Shine, Jesus, Shine

GRAHAM KENDRICK

GRAHAM KENDRICK

1. Lord, the light of Your love is shin - ing, In the
2. Lord, I come to Your awe - some pres - ence, From the
3. As we gaze on Your king - ly bright - ness, So our

midst of the dark - ness shin - ing; Je - sus, Light of the
shad - ows in - to Your ra - diance; By the blood I may
fac - es dis - play Your like - ness, Ev - er chang - ing from

world, shine up - on us, Set us free by the truth You now
en - ter Your bright - ness; Search me, try me, con - sume all my
glo - ry to glo - ry; Mir - rored here, may our lives tell Your

bring us; Shine on me. Shine on
dark - ness; Shine on me. Shine on
sto - ry;

REFRAIN

me. Shine, Je - sus, shine, fill this land with the Fa - ther's glo - ry; Blaze, Spir - it, blaze, set our hearts on fire. Flow, riv - er, flow, flood the na - tions with grace and mer - cy; Send forth Your Word, Lord, and let there be light.

22 Send the Light

CHARLES H. GABRIEL

1. There's a call comes ring-ing o'er the rest-less wave: "Send the
2. We have heard the Mac-e-do-nian call to-day:
3. Let us pray that grace may ev-'ry-where a-bound:
4. Let us not grow wea-ry in the work of love.

light! Send the light!" There are souls to res-cue, there are
And a gold-en of-f'ring at the
And a Christ-like spir-it ev-'ry-

"Send the light! Send the light!" Let us gath-er jew-els for a

souls to save. Send the light! Send the light!
cross we lay.
where be found.
crown a-bove.

Send the light! Send the light!

REFRAIN

Send the light,_____ the bless-ed gos-pel light. Let it

Send the light, the bless-ed gos-pel light.

shine_____ from shore to shore. Send the

Let it shine

from shore to shore.

light,_____ and let its ra - diant beams Light the

Send the light, and let its ra - diant beams

world_____ for - ev - er - more.

Light the world

for - ev - er - more.

Go

LEON PATILLO

23

LEON PATILLO
Arranged by Eugene Thomas

1. Go ye there - fore and teach all na - tions,
2. If you love_____ Me, real - ly love Me,
3. Go ye there - fore and teach all na - tions,

go, go, go. Go ye
feed My sheep. If you
go, go, go. Go ye

there-fore and teach all na - tions, go, go,
love Me, real - ly love Me, feed My
there-fore and teach all na - tions, go, go,

go. Bap - tiz - ing them in the name of the
sheep. Lo, I'll be with you for - ev - er and
go. Bap - tiz - ing them in the name of the

Fa - ther and Son, and Ho - ly Ghost.
ev - er, un - til the end of the world.
Fa - ther and Son, and Ho - ly Ghost.

Go, go, go.

Tell Me What to Do

24

STEPHEN R. ADAMS

STEPHEN R. ADAMS

1. Tell me what to do, tell me what to do,
2. Show Your will to me, Show Your will to me,
3. I am list-'nin', Lord, I am list-'nin', Lord,

Tell me what to do and I'll o-bey.
Show Your will to me and I'll o-bey.
Lord, I'm list-'nin', tell me what to do.

Tell me what to do, I give my life to You.
Show Your will to me, I'll do it will-ing-ly,
I am list-'nin',Lord, and lean-in' on Your Word.

Tell me what to do and I'll o-bey.
Show Your will to me and I'll o-bey.
Tell me what to do and I'll o-bey.

25

As Bread that Is Broken

PAUL BALOCHE and
CLAIRE CLONINGER

PAUL BALOCHE and
CLAIRE CLONINGER

1. Man - y hearts___ are hun - gry to - night,
2. Help us to___ be - gin where we are,

man - y trapped_ in dark - ness, yearn for___ the light; So
help us love___ the peo - ple near to___ our hearts; Then

man - y who___ are far from home___ and
give our faith___ a mis - sion field___ wher -

man - y who___ are___ lost, O
ev - er You___ may___ call, Lord,

Lord, Your wound - ed chil - dren need___ the
love Your world___ thro' each of us,___ un -

Cm7 Fsus F E♭/F
pow - er of Your cross.
til we've touched them all. As
REFRAIN
B♭ B♭/D E♭ B♭/D Cm
bread that is bro - ken, use our lives, as
F F/A E♭/G F/A B♭
wine that is poured out, a will-ing sac - ri - fice; Em -
B♭ B♭/D E♭ B♭/D Cm
pow - er us, Fa - ther, to share the love of Christ, as
B♭/F E♭/F Gm/F F B♭
bread that is bro - ken, Lord, use our lives.

26 Carry the Torch

DAVID BARONI and
LYNN KEESECKER

DAVID BARONI and
LYNN KEESECKER

We will car - ry the torch,_____ we will lift high the flame,_____ we will march thro' the dark - ness with the light of His name_____ un-til the glo - ry of God_____ is seen by the world._____ We will car - ry the torch_____ of_ the Lord.

car - ry the torch_____ of the Lord,_____

we will car-ry the torch___ of_ the Lord.

I Will Be Christ to You

27

MARTY PARKS

MARTY PARKS

I will be Christ___ to you,___ I will be Christ___

to you;___ I'll be His hands___ to

do what I can,___ Be-cause He has loved___ me,

too—___ I will be Christ___ to you.

28 Cross Every Border

GRAHAM KENDRICK

GRAHAM KENDRICK

1. We will cross ev - 'ry bor - der,
2. We will break sin's op - pres - sion,
3. We will gath - er in the har - vest,
4. Soon our eyes shall see His glo - ry,

throw wide ev - 'ry door, Join - ing our
speak out for the poor, An - nounce the
and work while it's day, Tho' we may
the Lamb, our ris - en Lord, When He re -

hands a - cross the na - tions, we'll pro - claim
com - ing of Christ's king - dom from east to west
sow with tears of sad - ness, we will reap
ceives from ev - 'ry na - tion, His blood-bo't Bride,

"Je - sus is Lord."
and shore to shore.
with shouts of joy.
His great re - ward. Then we'll pro - claim,

(continuation of previous hymn)

"Je-sus is Lord."   We shall pro - claim,   "Je-sus   is   Lord."

In Christ There Is No East or West   29

JOHN OXENHAM   ALEXANDER R. REINAGLE

1. In   Christ   there   is   no   East   or   West,   In
2. In   Him   shall   true   hearts   ev - 'ry - where   Their
3. Join   hands   then,   broth - ers   of   the   faith,   What -
4. In   Christ   now   meet   both   East   and   West;   In

Him__ no   South   or   North;   But__ one   great   fel - low -
high__com - mu - nion   find;   His__ ser - vice   is   the
e'er__ your   race   may   be;   Who__ serves   my   Fa - ther
Him__ meet   South   and   North.   All__ Christ - ly   souls   are

ship   of   love__ Thro' - out   the   whole   wide__ earth.
gold - en   cord__ Close   bind - ing   all   man - kind.
as   a   son__ Is   sure - ly   kin   to__ me.
one   in   Him__ Thro' - out   the   whole   wide__ earth.

30 The Ninety and Nine

ELIZABETH C. CLEPHANE

IRA D. SANKEY

1. There were nine - ty and nine   that   safe - ly   lay   In the
2. "Lord,____   Thou   hast here   Thy   nine - ty and   nine;   Are
3. But____   none   of the   ran - somed   ev - er   knew   How____
4. "Lord,____   whence are those blood - drops   all   the   way   That____
5. But____   all   thro' the moun - tains,   thun - der - riv'n,   And____

shel - ter____ of   the   fold.   But____ one____ was
they   not e - nough   for   Thee?"   But the   Shep - herd made
deep   were the wa - ters   crossed,   Or how   dark was   the
mark   out the moun - tains   track?"   "They were shed____ for
up   from the rock - y   steep,   There____ rose____ a

out   on the hills   a - way,   Far____ off   from the
an - swer: "This   of   mine   Has____ wan - dered a -
night   that the Lord   passed   thro'   Ere He   found   His____
one   who had gone   a - stray   Ere the Shep - herd could
cry   to the gate   of   heav'n,   "Re - joice!   I   have

gates____ of   gold;   A - way   on the moun - tains
way____ from   Me;   And al - though____ the road____ be
sheep that was   lost.   */   Out   in the des - ert He
bring____ him   back."   "Lord,   whence are Thy hands____ so
found____ My   sheep!"   And the an - gels ech - oed   a -

wild and bare, A - way from the ten - der Shep - herd's
rough and steep I go to the des - ert to find____ My
heard its cry– ᵧ Sick____ and help - less and read - y to
rent and torn?" "They're pierced____ to - night____ by man - y a
round the throne, "Re - joice, for the Lord____ brings back____ His

care, A - way from the ten - der Shep - herd's care.
sheep, I go to the des - ert to find____ My sheep."
die, ᵧ Sick____ and help - less and read - y to die.
thorn; They're pierced____ to - night____ by man - y a thorn."
own! Re - joice, for the Lord____ brings back____ His own!"

Hear the Voice of Jesus Calling   31

DANIEL MARCH, alt.

Gregorian Chant
Adapted by LOWELL MASON

1. Hear the voice of Je - sus call - ing, "Who will
2. If you do not cross the o - cean And a
3. If you can - not be a watch - man Stand - ing
4. Nev - er find your - self re - peat - ing, "There is

go and work to - day?____ Fields are white and har - vest
dis - tant land ex - plore,____ You can find the pa - gan
high on Zi - on's____ wall, Point - ing men to find the
noth - ing I can____ do;" While a world of men is

read - y; Who will bear the sheaves a - way?"
clos - er And the need - y at your___ door.
Sav - ior Who is life and peace to___ all,
dy - ing, There's a work God calls you___ to.

Loud and long the Mas - ter calls you; Rich re -
Tho' your tal - ents may be mea - ger, Of - fer
With your gifts and in - ter - ces - sions You can
Glad - ly take the task He gives you, Let His

ward He of - fers free. Who will an - swer, glad - ly
up the things you can; And what - e'er you do for
do as He com - mands, Join - ing with all faith - ful
will your plea - sure be; An - swer quick - ly when He

say - ing, "Here am I, send me, send___ me!"
Je - sus Will be use - ful in His___ hand.
spokes - men Serv - ing Him in dis - tant___ lands.
calls you, "Here am I, send me, send___ me!"

One of Your Children Needs You, Lord 32

MOSIE LISTER

MOSIE LISTER

1. One of Your chil - dren needs You, Lord.
2. One of Your chil - dren is cry - ing, Lord.
3. One of Your chil - dren loves You, Lord.

we give you Pra-ise and ho-nor Lord

One of Your chil - dren needs You, Lord.
One of Your chil - dren is cry - ing, Lord.
One of Your chil - dren loves You, Lord.

One of Your chil - dren needs You, Lord,
One of Your chil - dren is cry - ing, Lord,
One of Your chil - dren loves, You, Lord,

Je - sus, Je - sus, be near.
Je - sus, Je - sus, be near.
Je - sus, Je - sus, be near.

is Lord

33 Tell the Blessed Story

HALDOR LILLENAS   HALDOR LILLENAS

1. Church of God, a - wak - en; heed the Lord's com - mand.
2. Has He not com - mis - sioned you the news to bear?
3. Stand no long - er i - dle while the mo - ments fly.
4. Pub - lish un - to all the world re - deem - ing grace.

Tell the bless - ed sto - ry of the cross.   Fields are white for
Tell the bless - ed sto - ry of the cross.   "Go ye in - to
Tell the bless - ed sto - ry of the cross.   Mul - ti - tudes in
Tell the bless - ed sto - ry of the cross.   Un - til in the

har - vest - ing on ev - 'ry hand.
all the world," and ev - 'ry - where
hea - then dark - ness live and die.
home of rest you find your place,

Tell the bless - ed

sto - ry of the cross.

REFRAIN

Tell the bless - ed sto - ry of the

cross of Je - sus. Tell the bless-ed sto-ry of the

hal - lowed cross. Un - til ev-'ry na-tion learns of full sal -

va - tion, Tell the bless-ed sto-ry of the cross.

Ancient of Days

34

JAMIE HARVILL
and GARY SADLER

JAMIE HARVILL
and GARY SADLER

Bless - ing and hon - or,   glo - ry and pow - er

C
G2/B
Am
G2/B
Be un-to the An-cient of Days.
C
Dm/C
C
Dm/C
From ev-'ry na-tion, all of cre-a-
Dm/C
C
Am7
G2/B
C
-tion, Bow be-fore the An-cient of Days.
C
F
Dm7
G
Ev-'ry tongue in heav-en and earth
G
C/E
F
shall de-clare Your glo-ry, Ev-'ry knee shall

bow at Your throne_____ in wor - ship;

You will be_____ ex - alt - ed, O God,_____

And Your king - dom_____ shall not pass a - way,_____

O An - cient of Days._____

Your king - dom_____ shall

reign o - ver all the earth;

Sing un - to_____ the An - cient_____ of_____ Days!

For none can_____ com - pare to_____ Your

match - less worth; Sing un - to_____ the

An - cient_____ of_____ Days!

Let Your Heart Be Broken

35

BRYAN JEFFERY LEECH

JAMES MOUNTAIN

1. Let your heart be bro - ken For a world in need–
2. Here on earth ap - ply - ing Prin - ci - ples of love–
3. Blest to be a bless - ing, Priv - i - leged to care,
4. Add to your be - liev - ing Deeds that prove it true–
5. Let your heart be ten - der And your vi - sion clear–

Feed the mouths that hun - ger; Soothe the wounds that bleed;
Vis - i - ble ex - pres - sion God still rules a - bove,
Chal - lenged by the need Ap - par - ent ev - 'ry - where,
Know - ing Christ as Sav - ior, Make Him Mas - ter too:
See man - kind as God sees; Serve Him far and near.

Give the cup of wa - ter And the loaf of bread–
Liv - ing il - lus - tra - tion Of the Liv - ing Word
Where man - kind is want - ing Fill the va - cant place;
Fol - low in His foot - steps, Go where He has trod,
Let your heart be bro - ken By a broth - er's pain;

Be the hands of Je - sus, Serv - ing in His stead.
To the minds of all who've Nev - er seen and heard.
Be the means thro' which the Lord re - veals His grace.
In the world's great trou - ble Risk your - self for God.
Share your rich re - sourc - es– Give and give a - gain.

36

Lord, Let Me Serve

LINDA LEE JOHNSON

TOM FETTKE

Unison

1. Peo - ple are long - ing to learn of the Sav - ior;
2. Lord, let me serve wher - ev - er You need me.
3. Read - y and will - ing to give You my tal - ent.

Chil - dren are grow - ing,___ not know - ing He cares.
Make me a ves - sel___ thro' which You can flow.
Show me the task___ and I'll serve You to - day.

Lord, let me tell them a - bout Your com - pas - sion.
Give me a mis - sion, a place of ful - fill - ment.
Give me a pas - sion to work for Your glo - ry.

Lord, where can I be used?___
Lord, where can I be used?___
Lord, where can I be used?___

Lord, let me serve; Lord, let me fol - low. Give me a place and a pur - pose to fill. Teach me to serve; teach me to fol - low. Use me to do Your will.

37

Freely, Freely

CAROL OWENS

CAROL OWENS

1. God for - gave my sin in Je - sus' name; I've been
2. All pow'r is giv'n in Je - sus' name, In

born a - gain in Je - sus' name; And in
earth and heav'n in Je - sus' name; And in

Je - sus' name I come to you To share His

REFRAIN

love as He told me to. He said, "Free - ly,

free - ly you have re - ceived; Free - ly, free - ly

give._____ Go in My name and, be - cause you be -

lieve, Oth - ers will know that I live." _____

Lord, Lay Some Soul upon My Heart 38

LEON TUCKER

IRA D. SANKEY

Lord, lay some soul up - on my heart And love that

soul thro' me; _____ And may I al - ways

do my part To win that soul for Thee. _____

39 This Pair of Hands

FLOYD W. HAWKINS   FLOYD W. HAWKINS

1. These hands I give to Thee, my bless-ed Sav - ior, To
2. Com - pas-sion-ate Re-deem-er, Thou hast saved me; Thy
3. O God, Thou art the King of all cre - a - tion, The

do Thy will, what-ev-er love de - mands; Re -
match-less grace no mor-tal un-der-stands. When
moun-tains quake and move at Thy com-mands. Yet

deemed and sanc-ti-fied and in Thy fa - vor, I
cru - el, blight-ing sin had so en-slaved me, I
Thou hast planned, in bring-ing Thy sal - va - tion, To

glad - ly yield to Thee this pair of hands.
lift - ed to the cross this pair of hands. To
con - se - crate and use this pair of hands.

point the lost of earth to Cal - va - ry,   To

lift the cross that dy - ing souls may see,   To

bring Thy heal - ing touch to dark - est lands,   I

give to Thee, my God, this pair of hands.

Millennial Hymn

40

STEPHEN R. ADAMS

FRANZ JOSEPH HAYDN, alt.

1. Called to ev - 'ry cul - ture and na - tion, Sum - moned by God's
2. Called to serve wher - ev - er He leads us— That a need - y
3. When at last God's trum - pet calls us Home to Heav - en

Spir - it Di-vine. Called to live out truth's e - ter - nal, Shar-ing
world may_ know. We have heard that Great Com - miss - ion With_ an
we shall_ see Call - ing turned to shouts of tri - umph, Con - flict

hope and love's de - sign. This our priv - i - lege,___ this___ our
ea - ger - ness to__ go. By God's Spir - it,___ strength and__
raised to vic - to - ry. Far be - yond__ the__ cross__ of

Lord's com-mand,_ Love must_ go where need com-pels; Faith - ful is__ the
pow - er__ Heav - en's_ mes - sage we pro-claim! Christ has made us
sac - ri - fice,__ Crowns of__ life a - wait us all. Christ has made us

One who calls__ us, In Him__ all__ we__ need for ser - vice_ dwells!
more than con-quer-ors. We will__ tri - umph in His ho - ly__ Name!
more than con-quer-ors, Bless-ing and pow'r are__ in His heav'n-ly__ call.

Your Servant, Lord

41

STEPHEN R. ADAMS

CRAIG ADAMS

Your ser - vant, Lord, _____ I will be Your ser - vant,

Lord. The towel of sac - ri - fice, my ban - ner;

Your call-ing, my re - ward; _____ Your will, not

mine; _____ Sur-ren-dered to Your heart's de - signs. _____

Ev - 'ry day more like You, I will be Your ser - vant, Lord.

42

Shout to the North

MARTIN SMITH

MARTIN SMITH

1. Men of faith, rise up and sing of the great and glo - rious King, You are strong when you feel weak in your bro - ken-ness com - plete.
2. Rise up, wo - men of the truth, stand and sing to bro - ken hearts, Who can know the heal - ing pow'r of our awe - some King of love.
3. Rise up Church with bro - ken wings, fill this place with songs a - gain Of our God Who reigns on high, by His grace a - gain we'll fly.

REFRAIN
Parts

*(We will) Shout to the north and the south,

*Optional "We will"

sing to the east and the west; Je - sus is

1st time: D.C.
2nd time: continue
3rd time: Fine

Sav - ior to all, Lord of Heav - en and earth.

BRIDGE

Unison

We've been thro' fire,_____ we've been thro' rain,

We've been re-fined by the pow'r of His name; We've fal - len deep - er_____

in love with You, You've burned the truth on our lips.

D.C.

43 Little Is Much When God Is in It

KITTIE L. SUFFIELD   KITTIE L. SUFFIELD

1. In the har - vest field now rip-ened There's a work for all to
2. Does the place you're called to la - bor Seem so small and lit - tle
3. Are you laid a - side from ser - vice, Bod - y worn from toil and
4. When the con - flict here is end - ed And our race on earth is

do; Hark! the voice of God is call-ing To the har - vest call-ing
known? It is great if God is in it, And He'll not for - get His
care? You can still be in the bat - tle In the sa - cred place of
run, He will say, if we are faith-ful, "Wel-come home, My child– well

REFRAIN

you.
own.
prayer.   Lit - tle is much when God is in it! La - bor
done!"

not for wealth or fame. There's a crown– and you can

win it, If you go in Je - sus' name.

Surrendered, Completely Surrendered 44

STEPHEN R. ADAMS

STEPHEN R. ADAMS

Sur - ren - dered, com - plete - ly sur - ren - dered;

What - ev - er He wants, I'll o - bey.

Sur - ren - dered, com - plete - ly sur - ren - dered;

His will is my peace for to - day.

45 Bring Them In

ALEXCENAH THOMAS

WILLIAM A. OGDEN

1. Hark! 'tis the Shep-herd's voice I hear, Out in the
2. Who'll go and help this Shep-herd kind, Help Him the
3. Out in the des-ert hear their cry, Out on the

des-ert dark and drear, Call-ing the sheep who've
wan-d'ring ones to find? Who'll bring the lost ones
moun-tains wild and high. Hark! 'tis the Mas-ter

gone a-stray, Far from the Shep-herd's fold a-way.
to the fold, Where they'll be shel-tered from the cold?
speaks to thee, "Go find My sheep wher-e'er they be."

REFRAIN

Bring them in, bring them in, Bring them in from the fields of sin.

Bring them in,   bring them in,   Bring the wan-d'ring ones to Je - sus.

One Flock, One Shepherd
46

STEPHEN R. ADAMS

STEPHEN R. ADAMS

We are   one   flock,   one   Shep-herd;   The   sweet-est

sto - ry____ that has ev - er   been   told.   We   are

one   flock   led by   one   Shep - herd;   And

some - day   He   will   bring__ us____   to one fold.

47 Heart for the Nations

MARTIN J. NYSTROM
and GARY SADLER

MARTIN J. NYSTROM
and GARY SADLER

Give us Your heart for the na - tions, let us be light to the world; Use us to de - clare Your sal-va- tion to the peo - ple of the earth. May we be moved by com-pas - sion, let us know Your love for the lost; Lord, use us to lead them to the cross.

Fa-ther, here we are, stand-ing in Your pres - ence, Send us forth to lead them to the cross; Spir - it, here we are, fill us with Your pow - er, Send us forth to lead them to the cross.

48 Let the Lower Lights Be Burning

PHILIP P. BLISS   PHILIP P. BLISS

1. Bright-ly beams   our Fa-ther's mer - cy   From His light - house ev - er -
2. Dark the night   of sin has   set - tled, Loud the an   - gry bil - lows
3. Trim the fee - ble lamp, my broth - er!   Some poor sail - or, temp - est

more;   But   to   us   He gives the   keep - ing   Of   the
roar;   Ea - ger eyes are watch - ing, long - ing   For   the
tossed– Try - ing now   to make the   har - bor,   In   the

lights a - long   the   shore.
lights a - long   the   shore.   Let the low - er lights be
dark - ness may   be   lost.

REFRAIN

burn-ing!   Send   a   gleam   a - cross the wave!   Some poor faint - ing, strug-gling sea-man You may res-cue, you may save.

Not My Will, but Thine

49

HUGH C. BENNER

HUGH C. BENNER

Not my will, but Thine; not my will, but Thine; Not

my will, but Thy will be done, Lord, in me. May Thy

Spir-it di-vine fill this be-ing of mine. Not

my will, but Thy will be done, Lord, in me.

50 Reach the World

MARK BISHOP   MARK BISHOP

Unison

1. ⁷ It all starts____ with just one voice
2. One day that seed____ some-how breaks through.
3. A - cross the moun - tains,____ a - cross the sea,
4. Don't let me pray, Lord,____ for wealth or fame

That takes a stand,____ that makes a
Where there was one,____ there now stands
Soon oth - ers join____ in har - mo -
A spark that sets____ the world a -

choice   To live for God____ and not hes-i-
two.   And soon an - oth - er takes his__
ny.   They found the cross____ still stand-ing__
flame.   But help me reach____ the lost and a -

tate   To tell the world a - bout a - maz - ing
hand. A ray of hope that spreads a - cross__ the
strong. And soon a might - y cho - rus sings__ a -
lone, To tell of joy and hope where hope__ is

grace.
land.
long.
gone.

Go reach the world,_____ touch one more

soul, Bring one more lamb_____ back to the

fold. Each soul an - oth - er flag un -

furled. Each voice an - oth - er chance to reach_ the world.

INDEX